My Most Beautiful Dream

Мій найпрекрасніший сон

Bilingual children's picture book

Audiobook and video:

www.sefa-bilingual.com/bonus

Password for free access:

English: **BDEN1423**

Ukrainian: **На жаль, аудіокниги чи відео ще недоступні цією мовою. (Sorry, audio or video not yet available.)**

We are currently working on making as many of our bilingual books as possible available to you as audio books and videos. We kindly ask for your patience if there is no audio or video version in your language yet! You can keep up with the progress of our work on our website:
www.sefa-bilingual.com/languages

Cornelia Haas · Ulrich Renz

My Most Beautiful Dream

Мій найпрекрасніший сон

Bilingual children's picture book

Translation:

Sefâ Jesse Konuk Agnew (English)

Valeria Baden (Ukrainian)

Lulu can't fall asleep. Everyone else is dreaming already – the shark, the elephant, the little mouse, the dragon, the kangaroo, the knight, the monkey, the pilot. And the lion cub. Even the bear has trouble keeping his eyes open …

Hey bear, will you take me along into your dream?

Лулу не спиться. Усі інші вже бачать сни: і акула, і слон, і маленька мишка, і дракон, і кенгуру, і лицар, і мавпа, і пілот. І левеня. Навіть у ведмежатка заплющуються очі…

Гей, Ведмедику, візьмеш мене до свого сну?

And with that, Lulu finds herself in bear dreamland. The bear catches fish in Lake Tagayumi. And Lulu wonders, who could be living up there in the trees?

When the dream is over, Lulu wants to go on another adventure. Come along, let's visit the shark! What could he be dreaming?

І от Лулу в країні сновидінь ведмедя. Ведмедик ловить рибу в озері Тагаюмі. Та Лулу питає себе, хто би міг жити зверху на деревах? Сон закінчився, але Лулу хоче ще більше пригод. Давай навідаємося до акули! Що може їй снитися?

The shark plays tag with the fish. Finally he's got some friends! Nobody's afraid of his sharp teeth.

When the dream is over, Lulu wants to go on another adventure. Come along, let's visit the elephant! What could he be dreaming?

Акула грає з рибами у квача. Нарешті у неї є друзі! Ніхто не боїться її гострих зубів.

Сон закінчивя, але Лулу хоче більше пригод. Давай навідаємося до слона! Що може йому снитися?

The elephant is as light as a feather and can fly! He's about to land on the celestial meadow.

When the dream is over, Lulu wants to go on another adventure. Come along, let's visit the little mouse! What could she be dreaming?

Слон – легкий, як пір'їнка, і може літати! Ось він приземляється на небесну галявину.

Сон закінчився, але Лулу хоче ще більше пригод. Давай навідаємося до маленької мишки! Що може їй снитися?

The little mouse watches the fair. She likes the roller coaster best.
When the dream is over, Lulu wants to go on another adventure. Come
along, let's visit the dragon! What could she be dreaming?

Маленька мишка спостерігає за ярмарком. Найбільше їй подобаються американські гірки.

Сон закінчився, але Лулу хоче ще більше пригод. Давай навідаємося до дракона! Що може йому снитися?

The dragon is thirsty from spitting fire. She'd like to drink up the whole lemonade lake.
When the dream is over, Lulu wants to go on another adventure. Come along, let's visit the kangaroo! What could she be dreaming?

Дракона мучить спрага, бо він довго плювався вогнем. Він готовий випити ціле озеро лимонаду.

Сон закінчився, але Лулу хоче ще більше пригод. Давай навідаємося до кенгуру! Що може йому снитися?

The kangaroo jumps around the candy factory and fills her pouch. Even more of the blue sweets! And more lollipops! And chocolate!

When the dream is over, Lulu wants to go on another adventure. Come along, let's visit the knight! What could he be dreaming?

Кенгуру стрибає по кондитерській фабриці та набиває собі повну сумку. Ще більше синіх солодощів! І ще льодяників! І шоколаду! Сон закінчився, але Лулу хоче ще більше пригод. Давай навідаємося до лицаря! Що може йому снитися?

The knight is having a cake fight with his dream princess. Oops! The whipped cream cake has gone the wrong way!
When the dream is over, Lulu wants to go on another adventure. Come along, let's visit the monkey! What could he be dreaming?

Лицар влаштовує тортовий бій із принцесою своєї мрії. Ой, лишенько!
Повз пролітає вершковий торт!

Сон закінчився, але Лулу хоче ще більше пригод. Давай навідаємося
до мавпи! Що може їй снитися?

Snow has finally fallen in Monkeyland. The whole barrel of monkeys is beside itself and getting up to monkey business.

When the dream is over, Lulu wants to go on another adventure. Come along, let's visit the pilot! In which dream could he have landed?

Нарешті у країні мавп випав сніг! Уся мавпяча зграя з'їхала з глузду та вчинила балаган.

Сон закінчився, та Лулу хоче ще більше пригод. Давай навідаємося до пілота! У якому сні він приземлився?

The pilot flies on and on. To the ends of the earth, and even farther, right
on up to the stars. No other pilot has ever managed that.

When the dream is over, everybody is very tired and doesn't feel like going
on many adventures anymore. But they'd still like to visit the lion cub.

What could she be dreaming?

Пілот летить і летить. До краю землі та ще далі до зірок. Це не вдавалося жодному пілотові.

Коли сон закінчився, всі були втомлені й не хотіли більше ніяких пригод. Але до левенятка все ж вирішили навідатися. Що може йому снитися?

The lion cub is homesick and wants to go back to the warm, cozy bed.
And so do the others.

And thus begins …

Левенятко сумує за домівкою та хоче назад у своє тепле і затишне ліжко.

Та й усі інші також.

І тоді починається ...

... Lulu's
most beautiful dream.

... найпрекрасніший сон Лулу.

Cornelia Haas was born near Augsburg, Germany, in 1972. After completing her apprenticeship as a sign and light advertising manufacturer, she studied design at the Münster University of Applied Sciences. Since 2001 she has been illustrating childrens' and adolescents' books, since 2018 she is a professor for illustration at Münster University of Applied Sciences.

Корнелія Хаас народилася 1972 року неподалік від міста Аугсбург (Німеччина). Після навчання в Університеті прикладних наук у м. Мюнстер вона отримала диплом дизайнера. З 2001 року ілюструє книги для дітей та підлітків, з 2013 року є професоркою Університету Мюнстера за фахом „Акриловий та цифровий живопис".

www.cornelia-haas.de

Do you like drawing?

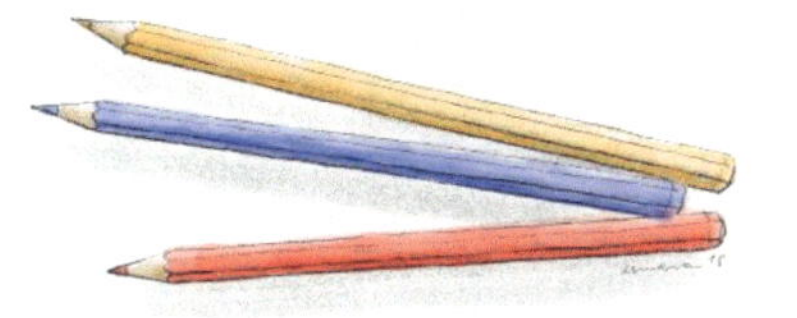

Here are the pictures from the story to color in:

www.sefa-bilingual.com/coloring

Enjoy!

Dear Reader,

Thanks for choosing my book! If you (and most of all, your child) liked it, please spread the word via a Facebook-Like or an email to your friends:

www.sefa-bilingual.com/like

I would also be happy to get a comment or a review. Likes and comments are great „Tender Loving Care" for authors, thanks so much!

If there is no audiobook version in your language yet, please be patient! We are working on making all the languages available as audiobooks. You can check the „Language Wizard" for the latest updates:

www.sefa-bilingual.com/languages

Now let me briefly introduce myself: I was born in Stuttgart in 1960, together with my twin brother Herbert (who also became a writer). I studied French literature and a couple of languages in Paris, then medicine in Lübeck. However, my career as a doctor was brief because I soon discovered books: medical books at first, for which I was an editor and a publisher, and later non-fiction and children's books.

I live with my wife Kirsten in Lübeck in the very north of Germany; together we have three (now grown) children, a dog, two cats, and a little publishing house: Sefa Press.

If you want to know more about me, you are welcome to visit my website: **www.ulrichrenz.de**

Best regards,

Ulrich Renz

Lulu also recommends...

Sleep Tight, Little Wolf

For ages 2 and up

Tim can't fall asleep. His little wolf is missing! Perhaps he forgot him outside?
Tim heads out all alone into the night – and unexpectedly encounters some friends …

Available in your languages?

► Check out with our „Language Wizard":

www.sefa-bilingual.com/languages

The Wild Swans

Based on a fairy tale by
Hans Christian Andersen

Recommended age: 4-5
and up

„The Wild Swans" by Hans Christian Andersen is, with good reason, one of the world's most popular fairy tales. In its timeless form it addresses the issues out of which human dramas are made: fear, bravery, love, betrayal, separation and reunion.

Available in your languages?

► Check out with our „Language Wizard":

www.sefa-bilingual.com/languages

More of me ...

Bo & Friends

▶ Children's detective series in three volumes. Reading age: 9+

▶ German Edition: „Motte & Co" ▶ www.motte-und-co.de

▶ Download the series' first volume, „Bo and the Blackmailers" for free!

www.bo-and-friends.com/free

IT: Paul Bödeker, Freiburg, Germany

ISBN: 9783739943633

Version: 20190101

www.sefa-bilingual.com

Made in United States
Troutdale, OR
06/15/2024

20586491R00026